Exciting things to do with nature materials

about this book

LOOK AND MAKE BOOKS are real do-it-yourself craft books. Every page has such clear step-by-step pictures and easy-to-follow words that you can do everything on your own without adult help. And once you see how the projects work, you'll be inspired to make dozens of creative things!

This book is about things you can make with natural materials that you find in the garden, in the countryside, by the seashore, or even in the kitchen.

The orange tag at the side of the page tells you what kind of natural objects are used for the projects in that chapter – all the projects between one tag and the next use the same, or similar, things.

The 'Try it first' tag at the top of the page indicates a practice section. This is included to help you understand how a method works with a simple project, before starting on something bigger and more exciting.

Before you start it's helpful to read through the 'Useful things to know' pages that follow.

Useful things to know

Going on a country walk

When you are out on a walk, stop from time to time to look around. See how many plants and trees you can recognize. Look out for signs and tracks of insects and animals. Try to protect the countryside. Don't destroy or dig up plants, and if you want to pick a wild flower make sure there are plenty more of the same kind in the area – and only take one.

Things to take with you

- ☐ Large shoulder bag
- ☐ 2 or 3 plastic bags and rubber bands to close them
- ☐ String, for tying twigs together
- ☐ Plastic containers with lids
- ☐ Wet cotton wool and foil for tying round plant stems
- ☐ Sketch pad and pencil
- ☐ Books for identification
- ☐ Scissors

Collecting

You can collect things at any time of year. Look for leaves and flowers in spring; leaves, flowers and seeds in summer; seeds and fruits in autumn and twigs, cones and husks in winter. You can find stones and shells in every season.

Flowers. Wherever possible use garden flowers for your projects. If you do collect wild flowers, make sure you choose only common ones. Remember there are poisonous plants about: try to make sure you know which these are.

Use scissors to cut the flowers, otherwise you may accidentally pull up the roots or damage the plant. The best time to gather flowers is early on a dry morning, after the dew has dried.

Leaves. If you want to preserve leaves in glycerine, the best time to pick them is early in the year,

Tools and materials

Dyes. Eggs, feathers and grasses can be dyed with fabric dye, available in powder or liquid form. Always wear rubber gloves and a smock or apron when you use dye; splashes won't come out easily. Follow package directions for mixing dye solution.

Eggs you want to eat should be dyed with vegetable food coloring, which you can buy in a supermarket. You will probably find it next to the cake decorations.

Paints. Poster paints are the most useful to buy for doing most of the projects. They are mixed with water and any spills can be cleaned up with water. You don't need to buy a whole range of colors: start with the basic ones – red, blue, yellow, black and white – and experiment with mixing.

Brushes. Buy two or three brushes, each of a different thickness. Use old lids, saucers or plastic egg-boxes for mixing the paints in.

Cardboard. The most useful backing for sticking things on, such as dried seeds, shells and flowers, is stiff board, such as Bristol board. If you are making a really big collage, like the one on pages 44 and 45, it is best to use a piece of Masonite. For small projects, cardboard, like the back of a writing pad, is quite strong enough.

Paper. Practice writing, printing and making cards with odd scraps of paper that you find around the house. For projects, use good quality drawing paper. It comes in various colors and weights.

Glue. White glue is the best all-round glue for these projects. You can also thin it with water to use as a varnish. If you splash some on your clothes, you must wash it out while it is still wet; once it is dry it won't come out.

Household cement is stronger than white glue, but is more expensive. Use it for making spots of glue which you want to dry very hard, very fast – such as for the stone animals or the twig mobiles.

when the sap is rising. Leaves picked in the autumn, when they have turned red and gold, will still drink the glycerine, but more slowly.

Collect leaves for printing at the end of the summer, when they have just fallen from the tree and are not yet dry and brittle. Try to find perfect leaves and avoid hard, shiny ones, like holly.

Seeding grasses. Collect these on a dry day at the end of the year, when they have already begun to dry out. Don't take more than you need or you may deprive some small animals of their food supply.

Twigs and branches. Never take even the smallest twig from a tree. Collect those which have fallen on the ground beneath the tree, or look for driftwood on the beach or by the river.

Shells. The most obvious place to find them is on the beach, but you may also find freshwater shells on the river bank. Make sure the shells are empty. Don't kill the creatures inside shells – there are plenty of empty ones around.

Feathers. You may be able to get large feathers, such as goose quills, from a poultry store. At the end of summer you may find feathers in the countryside, because this is the time when birds begin to molt.

Seeds from a grocery store are usually already dried. If you want to use fruit and vegetable seeds for your projects you must prepare them before you use them.
First wash the stickiness off with warm, soapy water and a scrubbing brush. Then spread the seeds on absorbent paper and leave them in a warm place to dry. Don't put them in the oven, or they will shrivel, nor in the sun, or they will bleach.

Eggs. Use ordinary hens' eggs for painting and blowing. Wild birds' eggs are not suitable and should not be disturbed.

Storing

Leaves and flowers should be stored flat, between sheets of absorbent paper.

Twigs, seeds, shells and feathers can be stored in boxes with lids.

Scissors. For most of your cutting ordinary household scissors will do. For very careful cutting it is better to use sharp, pointed ones. For cutting fabric, use pinking shears. You will need a penknife for stripping the bark off twigs.

Pencils are graded according to whether they are hard or soft. H and no. 3 are hard and B and no. 1 are soft. The most useful type is in between, but for drawing fine details use a hard one.

Other tools it is useful to have are an eraser, a pair of tweezers, a toothpick, an old dishpan, felt-tipped pens, tape and a box or a bag for scrap materials.

Books. There are paperback field guides available that are small enough to be carried in a pocket. If you want more detailed books for reference, consult your librarian.

Doing a project

Before you start a project, read through the whole chapter first, so you have a picture in your mind of what to do. Then get together all the things you need. Refer to these pages if it helps.

Clear yourself a large space and cover it with newspaper, so that it doesn't matter if you make a mess with paints, dyes or glue. Cover

yourself up, too, with an apron or smock. Have an old cloth handy so you can clean your hands as you go along. If you get paint on yourself wash it off immediately with warm water and detergent.

When you've finished, always clear up blobs of paint, dye and glue as soon as possible. Roll up the newspaper with the messy side inside and throw it away.
Take care to put lids and tops back on properly and to wash brushes, palettes and other things you have used for your project.
Don't throw away odd scraps of paper and cardboard or leftover seeds, grasses etc. You never know when you might need them for another project.

LOOK AND MAKE BOOKS use the metric system of measurement. Use a metric ruler or tape to measure your materials.

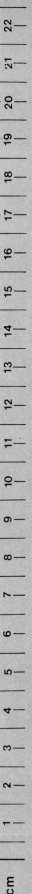

Pebble painting

If you enjoy collecting unusual stones you are called a rock hound – or perhaps a pebble pup if you are a beginner.

You can find stones in all sorts of places – in the garden or in the park, in the countryside or by the river. The best stones are the ones you find on the seashore, as they have usually been smoothed by the tides.

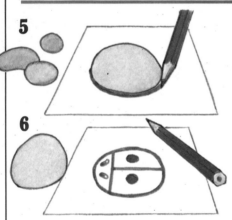

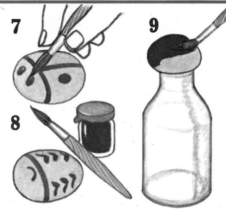

In the meantime, you could work out some designs.

5. Lay a stone on a sheet of paper and draw round it with a pencil.

6. Draw your design inside this pencil outline.

7. Using your drawn design as a guide, paint onto the stone with a fine paintbrush or a felt-tipped pen.

8. Wait for the paint to dry and then turn the stone over and paint the underside.

9. If you want to paint the stone all over in one color first, stand the stone on top of an empty bottle. Paint the top and the sides. When it is dry, turn the stone over and paint the last patch.

If you have chosen your stones for their interesting shapes, you can paint designs on them.

▶ You will need :
- ☐ Stones and pebbles
- ☐ Bowl of soapy water
- ☐ Nail brush
- ☐ Old, dry cloth
- ☐ Paper
- ☐ Pencil
- ☐ Poster paints and fine paintbrush
- ☐ Felt-tipped pen
- ☐ Varnish and brush (optional)

1. Put the stones into a bowl of warm, soapy water and scrub them with a brush. Scrub all the salt off stones from the beach and all the earth and grit off stones from the garden.
2. Rinse the clean stones under running water.

3. Rub each stone with a dry cloth.
4. Stand the stones on a window sill to dry out. Stones are porous, and hold moisture for a long time. Even when the surface looks dry there may be a little dampness left behind, waiting to seep out. This could spoil your painting, so leave the stones for a day or two before you paint on them.

Ladybug counters

Oval stones, like the two on the left, are perfect for making a set of counters for games. Try to find six that are more or less all the same size and shape.
Either paint your own designs on them, or paint them to look like the ladybugs above.
Paint each stone a different color all over. When they are dry, paint the spots, the eyes and the line of the wing-cases.

Give the stones a thin coat of varnish. Let it dry.
Give them a second coat.
When the second coat has dried, the surface of the stones will be glossy, and your design will not rub off.

Jar of shiny stones

When stones are wet, the colors are more striking than when they are dry.
If you have collected stones for their colors, store them in a glass jar full of water. They will make a nice decoration for your room. Add to your collection whenever you find unusual stones.

Dyeing grasses and flowers

Dried grasses have a soft, natural look, but if you prefer brighter colors, grasses are quite easy to dye.
Collect grasses late in the year, when they are beginning to dry out anyway. Pick the ones with really long stems and feathery seed heads.

3. Fill the net with hazel nuts or pebbles.
Tie the opening of the net into a knot.
4. Stand the net full of nuts with the knot underneath.
Arrange the grasses by pushing the stems down among the nuts.
Dried grass stems are very brittle, so treat them gently.

Dyeing from the outside

First dry the grasses. Tie the stems firmly together with string and hang them upside down in a warm, dry place for a few days.

▶ You will need:
☐ Dried grasses
☐ Rubber gloves and old newspapers
☐ Fabric dye
☐ Warm water
☐ Container and wooden spoon
☐ Vase or jar
☐ Hair dryer (optional)
☐ Coarse hairnet or net bag used for holding oranges
☐ Hazel nuts or pebbles

Before you start, put on rubber gloves, in case you get dye on your hands, and spread newspaper all over your work surface.

1

1. Stir the dye into warm water, following the instructions on the package. Prepare each color dye separately.
Dip the grasses into the dye, a few at a time.
Leave them in the dye until they are a deep color. Remember, they will dry a lighter color.

2

2. Lay the grasses on newspaper. This will absorb some of the moisture.
Then stand them upright in a vase or jar and leave them to dry in a warm room.
If you can blow-dry them with a hair dryer, they will dry more quickly and the seed heads will fluff up.

Dyeing from the inside

You can dye white flowers, such as chrysanthemums or carnations, by standing them in a dye mixture.

▶ You will need:
☐ Some white flowers
☐ Fabric dye
☐ Glycerine (from a drugstore) and warm water
☐ Tall container and wooden spoon
☐ Teaspoon

1. Mix the dye with two teaspoons of glycerine in the container.
2. Add warm water following the instructions on the package. Let the mixture cool.
3. When the mixture is cool, stand the flowers in it.

1
2
3

The flowers will drink the dye. In about an hour's time, they will have changed color. The longer you leave them in the dye, the deeper the final color will be. When the color is as strong as you want it, transfer the flowers to a vase or a bowl.

Scented bowls, bags and bundles

Many garden flowers and herbs are sweet scented. You can use some of them to make lovely-smelling sachets like the ones in the photograph.

You can buy dried flowers and herbs from a herbalist, but it's more fun to dry them yourself. If you dry them very carefully they will keep their scent for a long time. Remember always to ask permission before picking any flowers.

Rose bowl

▶ You will need:
- ☐ Two or three roses
- ☐ Pretty bowl
- ☐ Piece of cheesecloth

Pick the roses early in the morning, when they are just beginning to open.

1. Gently pull off the petals and spread them on the piece of cheesecloth. Then put the cloth, with the petals on it, into a closet, or some other warm, dry, dark place. Turn the petals over, very gently, once a day to help them to dry properly.

2. In about a week the petals should feel dry and slightly crisp. Then they are ready to be tipped into the bowl.

The delicate smell of roses should linger for many weeks.

1

Lavender bundle

▶ You will need:
- ☐ 9 or 11 long stems of lavender
- ☐ Yarn or embroidery floss
- ☐ Scissors
- ☐ Darning needle

1. Arrange the flower heads together and bind them with yarn. Finish off by tying the end of the yarn very tightly just below the heads.

1

2

Herb sachet

To make a sachet like the pink flowered one in the photograph

▶ You will need:
- ☐ Scented petals or herbs – roses, lavender or lemon balm, or a mixture of all three
- ☐ Piece of cheesecloth
- ☐ 2 squares of thin cotton fabric, at least 12cm x 12cm
- ☐ Needle, thread, pins
- ☐ Pinking shears

Dry the herbs in the same way as you dried the rose petals.

1. Pin the two squares of fabric wrong sides together and cut round the edges with pinking shears.

2. Stitch round three sides of the squares.

3. Tip the dried herbs into the open side.

4. Stitch the open side.

1

2

3

4

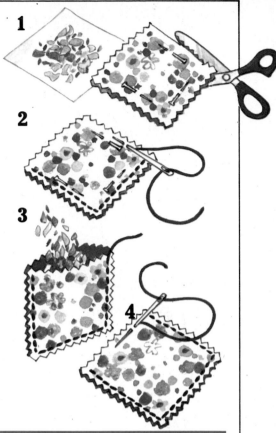

2

2. Bend all the stems upwards, so that they completely cover the flowers.

3   **4**

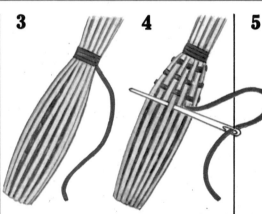

3. Tie one end of a long piece of yarn around the stems just above the lavender flowers.

4. Thread the other end of the yarn through the darning needle and weave the rest of the yarn in and out of the stems, until you reach the bottom.

5

5. Tie a knot in the end of the yarn and tuck it out of sight.
Trim the stalks, so that they are all the same length.

Herb sachets and lavender bundles make nice presents. Tuck them under your pillow or into drawers among your clothes to make them smell sweet.

Pressed flower presents

Collect some very common flowers and try pressing them.

The simpler the structure of the flower, or leaf, the better will be the result. Composite flowers tend to look squashed rather than pressed.

Once you have made a collection of pressed flowers, you could put them in an album, or you could use them to decorate cards.

▶ You will need:
- ☐ Common flowers
- ☐ Blotting paper
- ☐ Heavy books or a flower press

1. Arrange the flowers on a sheet of blotting paper, so that they do not touch each other.
Put another sheet of blotting paper on top.
2. Put several heavy books on top and leave them for about four weeks.

To use a flower press, like the one above, undo the screws and lift off the wooden top and one layer of cardboard and blotting paper. Lay the flowers down on the blotting paper. Replace the other piece of blotting paper, the cardboard and the wooden top. Tighten the screws as far as you can.
Screw the press as tight as you can.

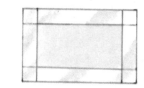

Decorated card

▶ You will need:
- ☐ Pressed flowers
- ☐ Card 10cm x 15cm
- ☐ Felt-tipped pen
- ☐ Transparent plastic wrap
- ☐ Scissors

1. Write your message on the card and arrange the pressed flowers around your message.

Cut a piece of plastic wrap slightly larger than the card on all sides.
2. Hold the plastic wrap firmly and press it down on the card.
Snip off the corners of the plastic.
3. Turn the edges under all round. Handle the plastic wrap very carefully. Any creases will spoil the arrangement.
You could make a bookmark or a picture in the same way.

Leaf prints and patterns

Fallen leaves are among the best natural things to print with. They are flat, have pretty shapes and delicate veins which, if you print really carefully, will show up quite clearly.
The leaf in the photograph was printed with green paint on white paper. You could use different colored paper or paint.

▶ You will need:
☐ Some different leaves
☐ Newspaper
☐ Paper to print on
☐ Poster paints
☐ Saucer and a little water
☐ Thick, stubby paintbrush
☐ Fine paintbrush
☐ Pencil

try it first!

1

2

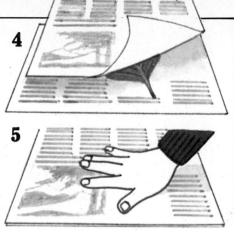

3

4

5

Spread newspaper all over the work surface in case you make a mess.
1. Powder paint should be mixed with a very little water in the saucer. Keep the paint as 'dry' as possible.
2. Starting with the leaf you like the least, cover the whole surface of the leaf with paint using the stubby brush. You can paint either the smooth or the veined surface.

3. Turn the leaf over and put the painted side on a sheet of newspaper.
Put it down firmly. Don't let it slide around or the print will be smudged.

4. Put another sheet of newspaper on top of the leaf.
5. Press down firmly with your hand. Make sure you press all over the leaf. Remember to press and not to rub.
Carefully lift off the top sheet of newspaper and the leaf and inspect your print.

1

2

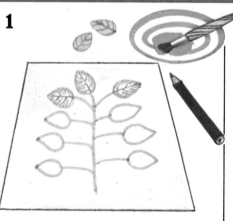

Leaf prints

When you have practiced a few times on newspaper try printing on good quality paper.
Print exactly as you did on the newspaper.

Picture making

If you use small leaves you can build up a picture. You could make a picture of a tree.
1. Draw the shapes lightly in pencil first. Print each leaf separately in position. You will probably be able to print more than once with the same leaf, but have some spares in case the leaf should tear.

2. Use a fine paintbrush and different colored poster paints to put in the branches.

Or make a picture using different kinds of leaves.

Leaves that last and last

A good way to preserve sprays of leaves is to stand them in a mixture of glycerine and water, as shown in the photograph on the left. The glycerine replaces the water in the leaves.

Beech leaves, clematis leaves and lily of the valley can be preserved particularly well this way.

Pick the sprays in the late spring or summer.

Christmas centerpiece

You could make a beautiful center-piece to decorate the table on special occasions such as Christmas day. Use the preserved leaves along with seed heads, everlasting flowers, cones and shiny balls.

▶ You will need:
- ☐ Preserved leaves
- ☐ Seed heads
- ☐ Dried flowers
- ☐ Evergreen leaves (such as holly)
- ☐ Cones
- ☐ Colored glass balls
- ☐ Trough-shaped dish or baking pan
- ☐ Wire mesh with 5cm gaps, or a lump of plasticine
- ☐ Newspaper
- ☐ Spray paints
- ☐ Drinking straws
- ☐ Christmas decoration (optional)

1

Cover your whole work surface with newspaper.

Lay the cones, some of the evergreen leaves and any other things you want to paint on the newspaper.

1. Hold the spray can about 10cm away from the objects and spray them all over.

2

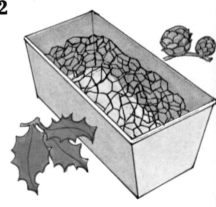

2. Crumple the wire mesh to fit inside your container. If you are using plasticine, press it firmly onto the base of the container.

1

▶ You will need:
☐ Sprays of leaves
☐ Narrow jar or vase
☐ Glycerine (from a drugstore)
☐ Water and spoon
☐ Ruler and string

Stand the leaf stems for a few hours in water.
1. Mix two parts of hot water to one part of glycerine and put the mixture into the jar or vase.

2   **3**

2. Crush the ends of the stems with the edge of the ruler.
This will help them drink the glycerine.

3. When the mixture is cool, stand the stems in it. Leave them there until the leaves have become supple and have changed color.
This may take between three days and three weeks.

4

4. When they are ready, tie the stems with string and hang them upside down for three days, so that the glycerine can reach the tips of the leaves.

3

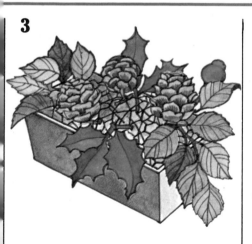

3. Arrange the leaves, the seed heads, dried flowers and cones, so that they overhang the container and hide it.

4

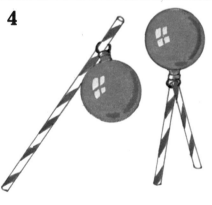

4. Finally, fix the balls on the drinking straws as shown and fix them in position.

If you like, add a Christmas decoration, such as a Santa Claus figure.

Fun with shells

If you go to the beach, you will probably collect shells.
Rare or beautiful shells should be kept just as they are – but there are all sorts of things you can do with the more ordinary ones.

▶ You will need:
☐ Some shells
☐ Saucepan of water
☐ Tweezers
☐ Newspaper
☐ Clear varnish
☐ Cardboard
☐ White glue and brush
☐ Poster paints and paintbrush
☐ Pencil
☐ Fine needle and thread (for necklace)

When you collect shells make sure there are no creatures inside.
1. Boil the shells in a saucepan. Then remove any bits left inside with tweezers.
2. Wash the shells thoroughly in hot soapy water and spread them on newspaper to dry.
3. Wet shells are more colorful than dry ones. To preserve a 'wet look' paint the shells with one or two coats of clear varnish.

scallop

nautilus

abalone

limpet

cowrie

mussel

16

Shell pictures

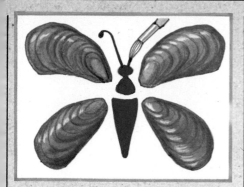

You can make pictures with shells by gluing them onto a piece of cardboard. Look at the shells you have found and see what pictures their shapes suggest.
Four mussel shells could look like the wings of a butterfly. Stick them in place on the card and paint the body and antennae with poster paints.

Shell initials

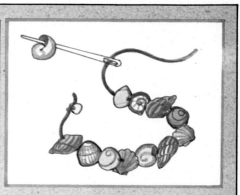

Ask whether you may glue a piece of cardboard to the door of your room; if so, you could make a plaque with your initial on it.
1. Draw your initial lightly in pencil on a piece of cardboard.
2. Spread glue all over the initial and stick down some small shells.

Shell necklace

Many shells have holes in them. You could thread small ones together to make a necklace or a bracelet.
Use a fine needle. If you force the needle through the shells they may split.

cockle

cowries

chiton

limpet

top shells

conch

murex

Shiny shells

One of the most attractive ways to use small shells is to glue them onto a box as decoration.
You could use lots of shells of the same kind, or you could use a variety of shells arranged in a pattern.

▶ You will need:
- ☐ Some shells
- ☐ Wooden box, or matchbox, to decorate
- ☐ Large sheet of paper
- ☐ White glue and brush
- ☐ Tweezers
- ☐ Pencil
- ☐ Clear varnish and brush

6

6. When the glue is completely dry, varnish over the whole surface. This will make the shells shine and help them to stay in place.

Think of other containers you could decorate in a similar way – glass bottles, empty yogurt pots, old jars.

Water garden

If you have some large, ornate shells you could make a water garden.

▶ You will need:
- ☐ Large glass jar or bowl
- ☐ Several large shells
- ☐ Sand
- ☐ Sheet of paper, scissors
- ☐ Freshwater plants (from pet shops)

1. Put about 3cm of sand in the bottom of the jar.
Wash the shells thoroughly and fill them with sand.
Arrange them on the sand in the jar with the insides facing upwards.
2. Cut a circle of paper to fit inside the jar and put it on top of your shell arrangement. This will prevent the sand from flying up when you pour water into the jar.

1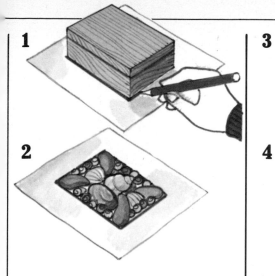

2

1. Place the box on the sheet of paper and draw around the base.
2. Arrange the shells in a pattern on the shape you have drawn.

3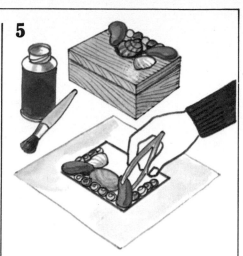

4

3. Dab glue on the center of the box.
4. Place a shell on the glued spot. You may find it easier to place shells with tweezers.

5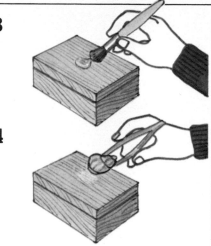

5. Following the pattern you made on the sheet of paper, glue all the rest of the shells onto the box, working from the center outwards.

1

2

3

3. Fill a container with water and gently trickle the water through your hand into the jar.
When the jar is full of water, remove the paper.

4

4. Push a freshwater plant into each shell so that the roots are embedded in the sand.

How to make a quill pen

Birds, like many other animals, molt, and their dropped feathers are very beautiful.

You can find feathers wherever there are birds – in gardens, parks or in the country – but *never* try to pull one from a living bird. If you can't find any feathers, ask your butcher if he has any he could give you. If you ever go to a zoo you may be able to collect some very bright feathers. On the other hand you can collect plain feathers and put them in fabric dye. The feather in the photograph was dyed in this way.

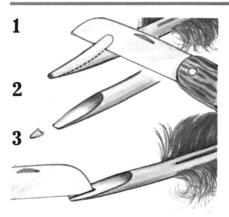

Put the feather, face downwards, on the cutting board.

1. Cut the feather at an angle, through the central shaft to the tip.

2. Cut off the very tip of the quill to make a straight edge for writing with.

3. Make a small cut down the center of the base of the shaft. This helps the ink flow properly.

► You will need:
☐ Feather
☐ Fabric dye
☐ Rubber gloves
☐ Bowl or dishpan
☐ Newspaper

The paler the feather, the better it will pick up the dye.
First wash it in warm, soapy water and rinse it thoroughly.
1. Put on rubber gloves and mix the dye with warm water in the bowl, following the instructions on the package.
Swish the feather to and fro in the dye for about ten minutes.
2. Rinse the dyed feather under cold running water.
3. Lay it on newspaper to dry out.
4. When the feather is dry, stroke it gently between your fingers to smooth it back into shape.
This is what birds are doing when they preen themselves.

shaft

base of shaft

Making a quill pen

► You will need:
☐ Feather, preferably from a goose
☐ Penknife
☐ Cutting board
☐ Ink
☐ Paper

The feather should be as perfect as possible. In particular the base of the shaft should be undamaged. It should have a hollow center at the tip.

You will find a quill pen quite difficult to use at first.
4. Dip the tip into the ink and scrape off any extra against the side of the ink bottle.
5. To start the ink flowing, you always have to begin a letter with a short sideways stroke.
Then you can make a down stroke. This will give your writing a very distinctive look.

When people wrote with quill pens their writing sometimes looked like this. Practice writing with your quill pen and copy the shapes of these letters.

abcdefghijklm
nopqrstuvwxyz
1234567890

Feather head-dress

You need quite a lot of feathers to make a headdress – and the more exotic they are the better will be the result.

Look at the fine headdress in the photograph. The large middle feather came from a hornbill; the other big feathers from the wings of turkeys and peacocks and the brightly colored feathers with the 'eyes' from a peacock's tail.

You may not be able to find such beautiful feathers. Don't worry. Collect as many as you can and look at them. Perhaps you can dye them. Or perhaps you will see that they look nice as they are. Even gray or brown feathers can look good, especially if they are speckled.

5

5. Dip the shaft of each feather in glue and slip it into place, following your arrangement, in a pocket of the tape.
Place each feather with its best side downwards.
You don't have to put a feather into every pocket, but make sure they overlap.
When all the feathers are in place, let the glue dry.

1

► You will need:
- [ ] Lots of tail or wing feathers
- [ ] About 100cm curtain tape, with drawstring if possible
- [ ] White glue, scissors
- [ ] Needle and thread
- [ ] Fabric paints and brush, colored tape or body feathers

1. Arrange tail or wing feathers: largest in the middle and the smallest at the sides.

2

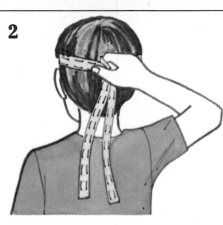

2. Put the curtain tape around your head so that it meets at the back. Hold the bit where it joins between your finger and thumb.

3

4

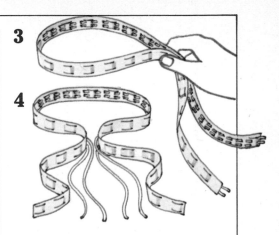

3. Take the tape off your head, still holding it together with your finger and thumb.
4. Unthread the drawstrings from each end of the tape up to your finger and thumb.
You will be able to use the two loose pieces of drawstring to tie the finished headdress in place.
(If you cannot get curtain tape with a drawstring, trim pleater tape to 4–5cm width. Sew on 20cm yarn or string ties.)

6

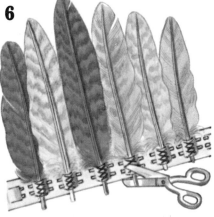

Sew the feathers to the tape. Use big stitches that criss-cross over the shafts of the feathers.
6. Trim the pointed ends of the feathers with a pair of scissors.

7. Turn the headdress over and decorate the band. If you have some small body feathers, you can glue them onto the band. Start at one end of the tape and glue the feathers on sideways so that they overlap each other.
8. Or you could decorate the band by sticking brightly colored tape along it.
9. Or you could paint the band with fabric paints. A bold simple design looks best.

When the band is decorated the finished headdress is ready to be tied on.

7

8

9

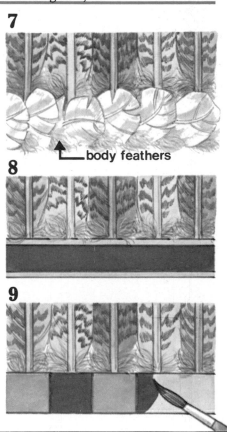

body feathers

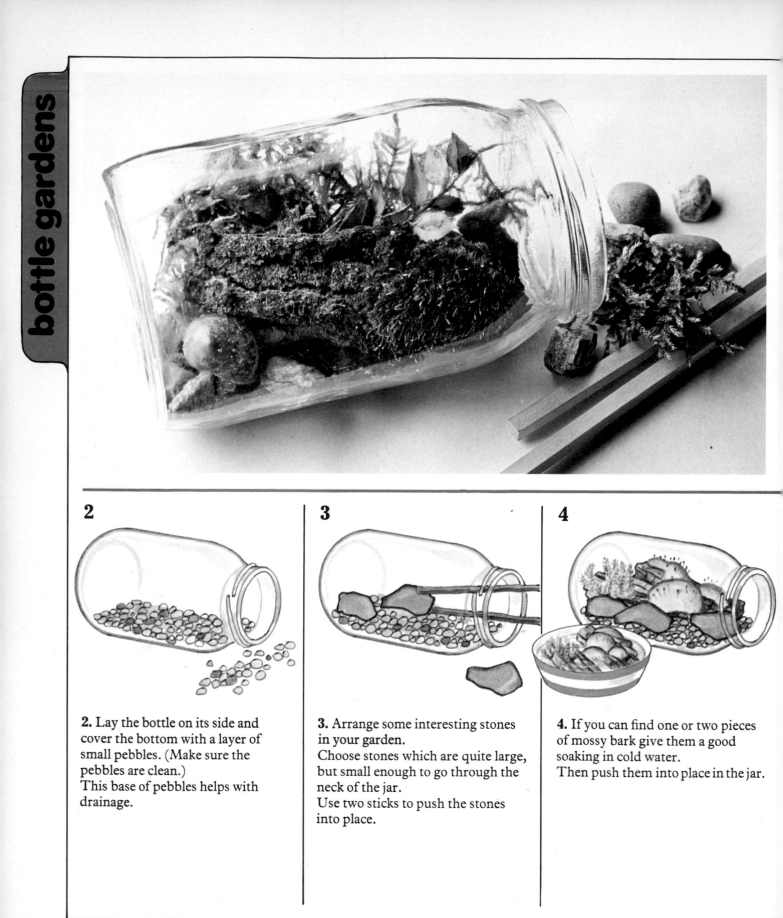

2. Lay the bottle on its side and cover the bottom with a layer of small pebbles. (Make sure the pebbles are clean.)
This base of pebbles helps with drainage.

3. Arrange some interesting stones in your garden.
Choose stones which are quite large, but small enough to go through the neck of the jar.
Use two sticks to push the stones into place.

4. If you can find one or two pieces of mossy bark give them a good soaking in cold water.
Then push them into place in the jar.

Stone and bark garden

A bottle garden is a complete world which needs hardly any attention once it has been planted. If the garden is damp, and the bottle you use has curved sides, moisture collects on the inside of the glass and 'rains' on the plants.
It is best to use a large bottle with a wide neck for your garden, but you can use a jam jar if you turn it on its side. Use a clear glass jar, because the plants need light. Colored glass will do if it is only slightly tinted.

For your first garden, put in stones and pieces of bark. The bark in the photograph has moss and ivy growing on it.

▶ You will need:
☐ Bottle with wide neck
☐ 2 sticks long enough to reach to the end of the bottle
☐ Clean pebbles and several larger stones and a small shell
☐ Bark with moss, ivy, or ferns on it
☐ Piece of sponge
☐ Strong twine
☐ Spray bottle
☐ Dish mop or brush

1. Clean the bottle very thoroughly with hot water and detergent. Scrub the corners with a brush. Rinse the bottle several times in clean water.

5

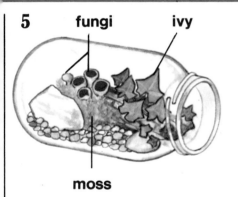

fungi   ivy

moss

5. Try to find a piece of bark with a little ivy growing on it.
If you are lucky these tiny plants will continue to grow in the greenhouse conditions of the bottle.
You may see that the bark has things growing on it that you didn't notice at first – tiny fungi, perhaps.

6

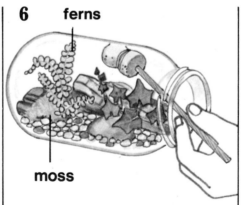

ferns

moss

If moss is growing in your bottle you should allow drops of moisture to form on the inside of the glass because this helps to keep it healthy.
6. If the glass gets dusty or cloudy inside you can clean it, using a small piece of sponge tied with twine to the end of a stick.

7

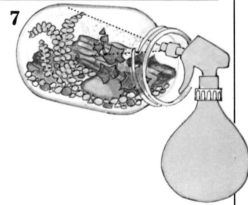

If your garden only contains some stones and bark it will not need to be watered at all. But if anything is growing in it, it will.
7. When it looks dry, water it with a spray.

On the next page you will see how to plant a bottle garden with growing plants.

Living plant garden

A stone and bark bottle garden like the one on the previous page is fun but, if you're feeling more ambitious, you could try a more elaborate one with plants that grow. It doesn't have to be quite as big as the one in the photograph.

▶ You will need:
- [ ] All the things listed under 'Try it first'
- [ ] Potting soil – buy sterilized potting soil. Garden earth can contain diseases which kill plants
- [ ] Cardboard tube
- [ ] 2 more sticks
- [ ] Old fork and spoon
- [ ] Small plants – ivy and ferns are best
- [ ] Plate
- [ ] Cork to fit the bottle top, or a saucer

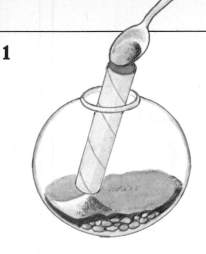

1

Wash the bottle and cover the bottom with pebbles as you did for the stone and bark garden.

1. Spoon the soil into the bottle through the cardboard tube. This will prevent the sides of the jar from getting dirty.

2

2. It is not easy to rearrange the plants once they are in the garden, so plan your garden on a plate first.
If you want to use stones and bits of wood, arrange them among the plants on the plate. Don't overcrowd the arrangement. Plants need space to grow.

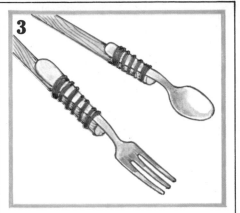

3

3. You might decide to pile the soil in your bottle into a hill, and to arrange the plants at different heights. You will need a fork and trowel to help do this.
Make these tools by tying the fork and spoon to the end of two sticks with twine.

4

4. When you are happy with your plan, start putting things carefully into the jar.
If you are going to use any stones or bark, put these in place first.
If the plants are in peat pots you can leave them in. If they are in clay or plastic pots tap the pots gently and tip the plants out.

5. Now put in the plants, one by one. Start by planting at the edges. Make a little hole with the spoon in the place where you want the first plant.
6. Push the plant, very gently, through the neck of the bottle. Hold it with the two sticks.
7. Use the spoon and fork, or the two sticks, to push the plant into the hole. Then push a little earth around the roots. Don't worry if you can't do this very successfully.

Plant all the rest of the plants in the same way. Try not to get impatient. Treat the plants very gently. If you can't push them to exactly where you want them, better to leave them than risk damaging them.
When the garden is finished, spray it thoroughly. Cover the neck of the bottle with a cork or a saucer. Spray the garden when it looks dry.

5

6

7

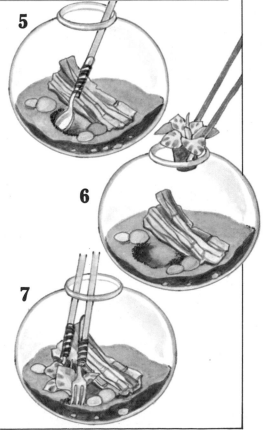

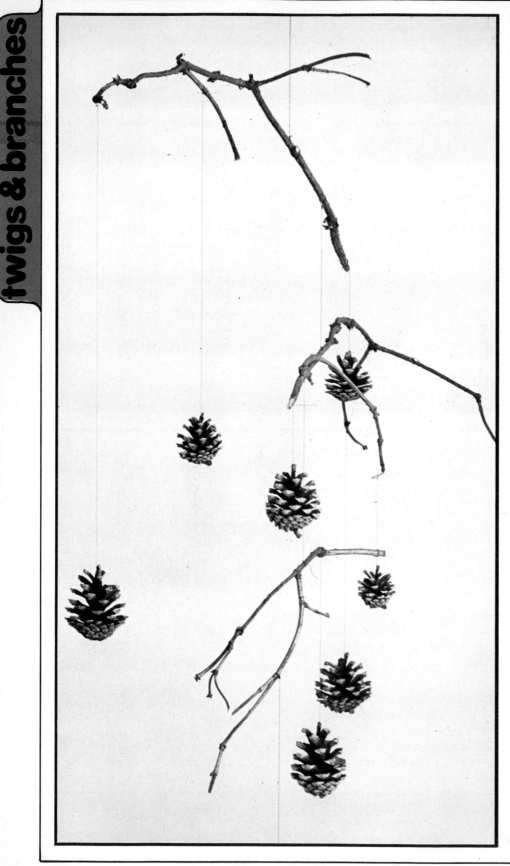

Twig mobiles

You can make a very effective
mobile with pine cones and twigs,
like the one in the photograph.
If you haven't any pine cones you
can use blown eggs, shells with
holes in them or dried flower heads
instead.
A mobile should be very light so
that the slightest draft will move it.
Choose light twigs with two or
three branches. These are
interesting to look at.
Don't use dry twigs as they may
snap: use strong twigs that bend
easily.

Twig mobile

▶ You will need:
☐ Strong twigs with several
   branches
☐ Thread
☐ Tape
☐ Pine cones or other light objects
☐ Glue

Tie one end of a long piece of
thread to one of the twigs. It
doesn't matter where you tie it,
because you can move it later.
1. Stick the other end of the thread
to the edge of a table or desk with
tape. Make sure the twig hangs
well above the ground.
Cut several pieces of thread. Tie
the end of each one to the top of a
pine cone and glue the knots.
2. Tie one of the pine cones to one
end of the twig, using a fairly loose
knot. The cone will make the twig
tilt to one side.

try it first!

Make a practice mobile on a wire coat hanger.

▶ You will need:
- ☐ Wire coat hanger
- ☐ Four or five seed heads, blown eggs, shells or dried flower heads
- ☐ Thread
- ☐ Glue

Hang the wire coat hanger on a hook or over a door handle while you are making the mobile.

1. Tie one end of a long piece of thread firmly to each object.
2. Put a drop of glue on each knot to make them even firmer.

1

2

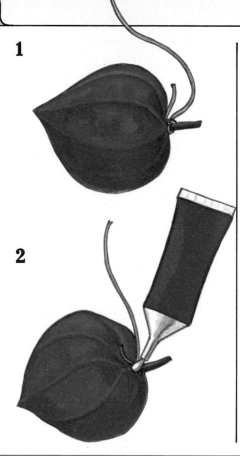

3

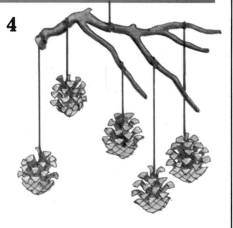

3. Now tie the other end of the threads to the coat hanger. Practice arranging them at different heights. Move the threads about along the hanger until it hangs level and does not tip to one side or the other.
Don't tighten the knots or cut off the ends of the threads until the mobile balances properly.

1

2

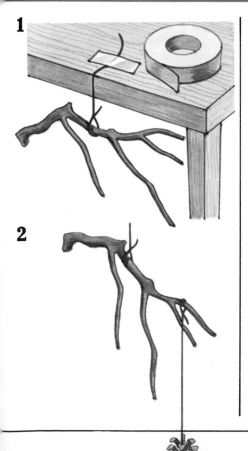

3

3. Tie another cone to the other end of the twig, and a third one near the middle. Tie on more if you want to. Make sure all the cones hang at different heights.
Now slide the threads along the twig until the mobile balances perfectly. If you need to, move the piece of thread which is holding the twig.

4

4. When you are pleased with your design and are sure that it will move well in a breeze, tighten all the knots, including the one holding the twig. Put a dab of glue on each one. Hang the mobile in a doorway or from a lampshade.
If you want to make a bigger mobile, tie thread round a larger twig and tape it to the table.
Tie the mobile to the new twig. Balance it by tying on more cones.

Turning branches into animals

Look at pieces of driftwood, or at twigs or small branches that have fallen from trees. Often you will notice that the natural shape looks rather like an animal or a bird. If you alter this shape slightly you can often create an exciting piece of sculpture.

Keep your ideas simple. They are not only easier to carry out, they also look better when they are finished.

The secret is to search hard until you find a piece of wood that already looks very like some creature. That way, most of the work has been done for you by nature.

Look at the dachshund and the peculiar bird in the photograph. You can see what the original twigs must have looked like before they were sanded down and varnished.

1

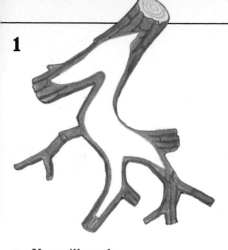

▶ You will need:
- [ ] Piece of wood and saw
- [ ] Penknife
- [ ] File
- [ ] Chalk and pencil
- [ ] Sandpaper
- [ ] Clear varnish and brush
- [ ] Plasticine for stand

1. Look at the wood and imagine the creature inside the shape.

2

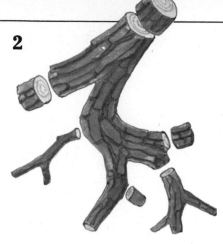

Can you see how the shape of twig above could be made into a stork?
2. Mark in chalk the places where bits of wood must be cut away.
Use a saw, or ask someone to cut these bits off for you, at the marks you have made.

3

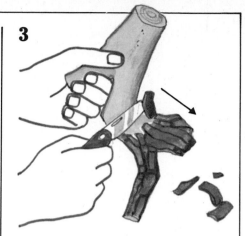

3. Strip off the bark with the penknife. Always scrape away from you, *never* towards you. If some patches of bark won't come off, leave them. The patchy look can be very effective.

4

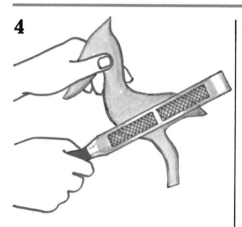

4. If you like, you can shape the details with the file. Keep the shapes simple.
To make the stork, all you would have to do would be to file his beak and tail into points.

5

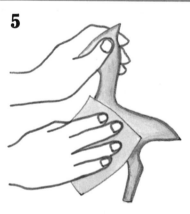

5. Smooth the whole creature by rubbing him down with sandpaper. Dot the eye with a pencil.

6

6. Shape some plasticine into a block and wedge the creature into it so that it stands upright. Paint the creature with clear varnish.

Sweet-smelling pomander

In sixteenth-century England, people carried pomanders, hoping the scent would protect them from the plague. Nowadays there is no plague to keep at bay, but a pomander will discourage moths and it makes a lovely present. Put it among the sheets or clothes in a drawer and they will smell beautiful.

The orange will never rot away, but as it gets older it will dry up and become smaller and harder. Some very old pomanders are no bigger than a walnut.

5

5. Sprinkle the cinnamon powder onto the tissue paper. If you have some orrisroot powder, sprinkle that on top of the cinnamon.
Mix the two powders together. The orrisroot powder is a fixative. This means that it fixes the scent of the orange and the cinnamon and makes it last.

6

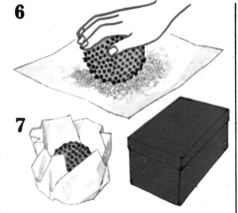

7

6. Roll the pomander over and over in the powder, until most of the powder has disappeared.
7. Wrap the pomander in the tissue paper and put it in an air-tight tin. Don't peek in, or the orange may go bad. In about three weeks, the orange will have dried and the pomander will be ready.

1

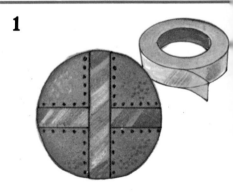

Decorated pomanders

As well as the things under 'Try it first' you will need narrow ribbon, some tape the same width as the ribbon, some sequins and white glue.
1. Wrap tape round the center of the orange, in both directions, as shown.
Pierce holes along each side of the tape and push a clove into each one.

try it first!

▶ You will need:
- ☐ Large fresh orange
- ☐ Jar of whole cloves
- ☐ 2 teaspoons of powdered cinnamon
- ☐ Round toothpick
- ☐ Tissue paper
- ☐ Air-tight tin
- ☐ 2 teaspoons of orrisroot powder from the drugstore (you can leave this out, but it does help the scent last longer)

1. Make a ring of holes around the middle of the orange with a toothpick.
2. Push a clove, pointed end first, into each hole.
Push the cloves in so that only the heads stick out.
The cloves should be close together, almost touching.

1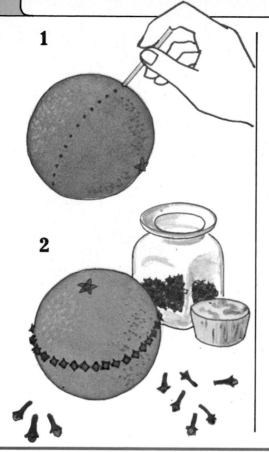

2

3 **4**

3. Now make another ring of holes above the first one. Make each new hole above the space between the first holes.
Push a clove into each hole.
Go on making rings of holes and pushing in cloves until the top half of the orange is covered.
4. Then cover the bottom half of the orange in the same way.

2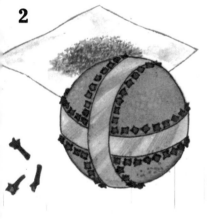

2. Cover the rest of the orange with cloves, in the same way as before, except for the taped parts.
Roll the orange in cinnamon and orrisroot powder.
Leave it to dry for three weeks.
Then remove the tape.

3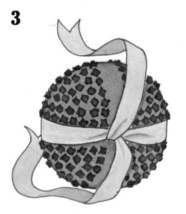

3. Now tie the ribbon around the orange, in the channels you made for it.

4

4. Tie a bow at the top end.
If you have any sequins you can glue them onto the ribbon to make it glitter.

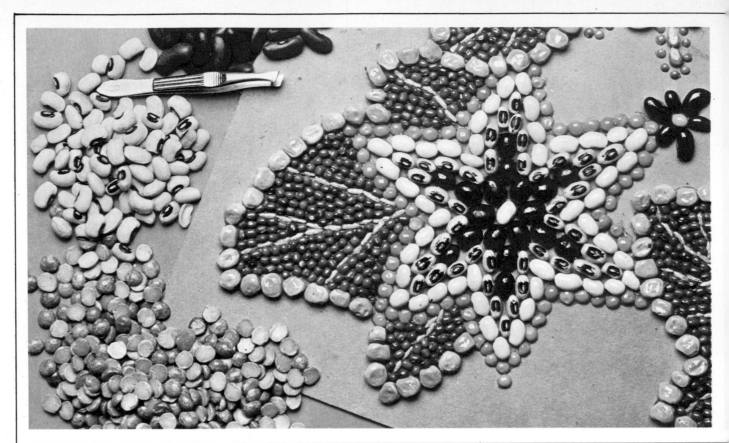

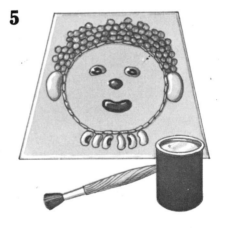

Use your pattern of loose seeds as a guide, and glue the seeds you had put to one side on the cardboard.

3. The glue will dry quickly, so use the toothpick to spread just a little at a time on the cardboard.

4. Pick up the seeds one by one with tweezers and press them on the glued patch.

Spread a little more glue and do the next bit of the pattern.

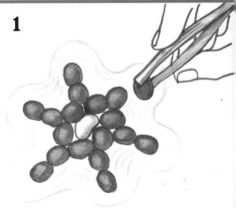

5. When your seed picture is quite dry, paint over it with varnish.

Paint the board as well as the seed picture.

The varnish will make the seeds stick to the board even more firmly. It will also give them a lovely glossy shine.

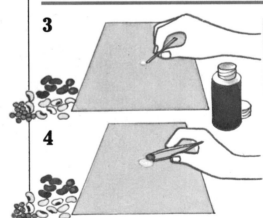

Flowers and leaves

Once you have practiced making simple patterns, you could try a pattern of flowers and leaves like the one in the photograph. It doesn't matter if you don't use the same seeds as the ones shown.

1. Start with the star-shaped flower. Glue a white seed in the center. Then arrange brown seeds in a star shape around it.

Pictures with seeds

The photograph on the left shows some of the different peas and beans you might find in the kitchen cupboard.

White ones include pea beans, lima beans, rice and barley. Yellow ones are yellow split peas and popping corn. Green ones are green split peas, green lentils and mung beans. Red ones are kidney beans. Brown ones are coffee beans and brown lentils. Black-eyed peas are white with black eyes! Ask if you can use some of each kind to make patterns and pictures.

1

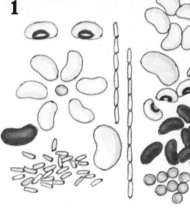

▶ You will need:
☐ Some beans, peas and grains
☐ Paper
☐ White glue
☐ Toothpick and tweezers
☐ Clear varnish and brush
☐ Pencil
☐ Piece of stiff cardboard

1. Spread out the seeds. What do the shapes look like? Are black-eyed peas eyes? Are beans ears?

2

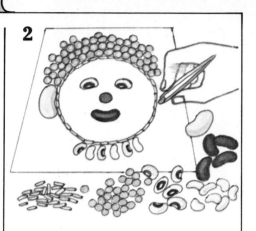

Put half your seeds to one side.
2. Arrange the other half of the seeds in a pattern you like on a sheet of paper. If your fingers are too clumsy for the smaller seeds, use the toothpick, or tweezers, to push them into place. It's best to start with a very simple pattern.

2

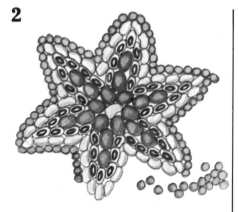

2. Arrange three more rows of seeds of contrasting colors around the star shape. Make sure all the seeds touch one another.

3

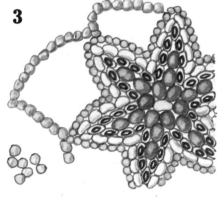

3. Now make the leaves. Outline the shape of the leaves with large green seeds, such as dried peas.

4

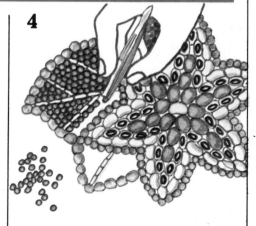

4. Then glue down lines of rice or barley to make the veins.
Fill in the spaces between the veins with small green seeds, such as mung beans or split peas.

Because there are different ways of decorating eggs you won't need all these things – only those for the ways you want to try.

▶ You will need :
- [ ] Some eggs
- [ ] Onion skins
- [ ] Scraps of cloth
- [ ] Thread
- [ ] Saucepan of water
- [ ] Eggcup
- [ ] Paintbrush
- [ ] Vegetable food coloring
- [ ] Poster paints
- [ ] Colored felt-tipped pens
- [ ] Wax crayons
- [ ] Fabric dyes
- [ ] Warm water
- [ ] Container and wooden spoon
- [ ] Teaspoon

Colorful eggs

There are a lot of different ways you can decorate eggs. You can paint them with felt-tipped pens, like the patchwork egg in the photograph. Or you can draw on them with wax crayons and dye them, like the other eggs in the photograph.

White eggs are the easiest to paint because the colors show up better. But brown eggs look nearly as nice.

Eggs have porous shells and it is just possible that some of the color might seep through a thin shell onto the egg. So if your painted eggs are to be eaten, use vegetable food coloring. You can buy it in supermarkets in several colors.

If you are going to eat a decorated egg, don't keep it for more than about three days.

1

Paint and felt-tip pens

If you want to keep your decorated eggs, rather than eat them, they need to be hard-boiled for at least half an hour. The eggs will keep for a long time and they will be quite durable.

1. Try painting patterns on them with poster paints.

1 **2**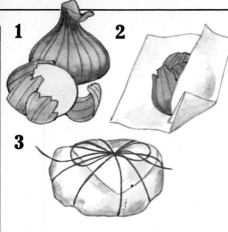

3

4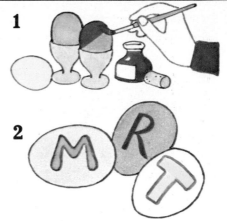

5

1 **2**

Marbled eggs

1. Wrap some raw onion skins carefully around the egg.
2. When the egg is covered with onion skins, wrap the whole thing in a piece of cloth.
3. Tie thread firmly around the parcel.

4. Hard-boil the wrapped egg. When the egg is cooked, leave it to cool.
5. Unwrap the parcel and peel off the onion skins. The egg will have a beautiful pattern, like marble, all over it.

Dyeing eggs

If you are taking hard-boiled eggs on a picnic, why not paint each one differently? Then everyone can recognize his or her own rations.
Make sure the egg is quite dry. Stand it in an eggcup.
1. Use vegetable food coloring to paint each egg a different color.
2. Or paint on the right initials.

2

3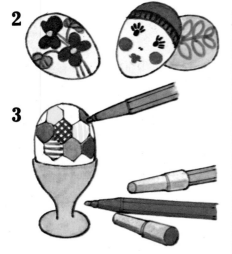

1

2 **3**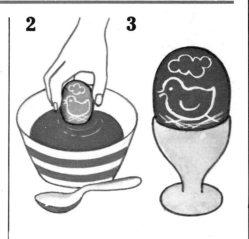

2. You can paint one color on top of another if you let the first color dry before starting on the second.
3. You can draw on the egg with felt-tipped pens too, like the patchwork egg in the photograph. Don't press too hard or the tip may go through the shell.

Using wax crayons

To decorate eggs like the ones in the photograph you will need wax crayons and fabric dye. Mix the dye following the instructions on the package. Make sure that the color of the crayon contrasts with the color of the dye.
1. Draw a pattern with wax crayon on the hard-boiled egg.

2. Put the egg into the dye. Take it out from time to time to see how strong the color has become. When it is a deep color put the egg in an eggcup to dry.
3. The dye will not have 'taken' where the wax lines are and your drawing will show clearly.

Hollow eggs

Hard-boiled eggs are nice to decorate, but once you have learned how to blow eggs you can do even more exciting things with them.

▶ You will need :
- ☐ Eggs
- ☐ Eggcup
- ☐ Darning needle
- ☐ Small wooden board
- ☐ Thin nails
- ☐ Hammer
- ☐ Bowl
- ☐ Poster paints and paintbrush
- ☐ Used match (broken, if large) and thread

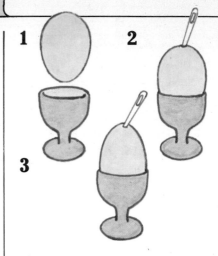

1. Place an egg in an eggcup, pointed end downwards.
2. With the point of the darning needle, pierce a hole in the top of the egg. It won't crack if you do this very gently.
Turn the egg the other way up.
3. Pierce a hole in the pointed end of the egg. Move the needle around inside this hole to make it a little larger than the other one.

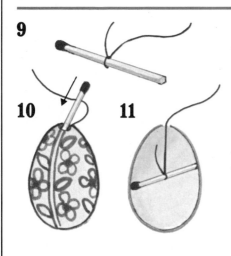

You can hang up a finished egg as a decoration.
9. Tie a piece of thread to the middle of a used match.
10. Push the match into the larger of the two holes.
11. The match will stay firmly in place and you can hang the egg by the piece of thread.

Christmas decorations

You can hang your finished eggs on a Christmas tree.

Hanging eggs

Or hang them from a picture hook in your room. Or make them into a mobile.
They will look their best if all the pieces of thread are of different lengths.

4

5

6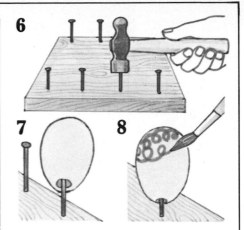

7 **8**

4. Hold the egg over a bowl. Put your mouth against the smaller hole and blow. The insides of the egg will come out of the larger hole into the bowl.
If the insides won't come out, shake the egg and blow again. Or push the needle into the hole and wiggle it around.
Someone can use the insides of the egg for cooking.

5. Clean the inside of the egg thoroughly, or it will smell.
Hold the egg under the tap so that the water runs in through one hole and out of the other. Shake the egg to dry it out.
Remember that you must be very gentle indeed, or you will break the fragile eggshell.

Make a special egg stand.
6. Hammer some thin nails into a board. Hammer them in just enough to hold them in place.
7. Put each egg on a nail, so that the nail goes into the larger hole.
8. Paint each egg on its nail and leave it there to dry.

1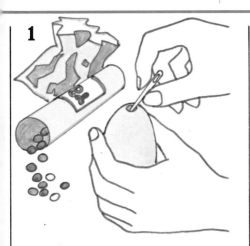

2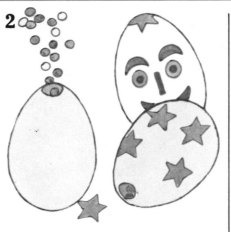

Presents

You can put something inside a blown egg to make a surprise present.

1. First, make the hole in the pointed end of the egg bigger. Move the needle carefully around the edges of the hole.

2. Fill the egg with very tiny candies. The smaller and lighter the candies are, the less chance there is that the egg will crack. Decorate the egg with gummed paper shapes. Stick the last shape directly over the hole.

Finger puppets

You can turn blown eggs into finger puppets.
Enlarge the hole in the pointed end, until it is big enough for you to put your finger inside.
Paint a different face on each egg and give your own puppet show.

mouse-drawn cart

stone animal

Nature parade

With a bit of imagination you could use some of the odd stones, shells and grasses you have collected to make some curious creatures like the ones in the photograph.
Once you have tried out these ideas think of some other creatures you could make – such as a shell frog, a stone owl, a leaf butterfly or a grass spider.

Mouse-drawn cart

You could have fun making a cart like this with vegetables and fruits from the kitchen. You could use it as a table decoration, or present it to someone as a sculpture to eat.
If you don't want it to get disturbed, make it up on a large plate.

▶ You will need:
- [ ] Orange
- [ ] Cucumber
- [ ] 3 radishes
- [ ] 8 cloves
- [ ] Carrot
- [ ] Scallion
- [ ] Kitchen knife
- [ ] Used matchstick
- [ ] Large plate

The cart

1. Cut the orange in half and put one half down for the cart. Cut four thick slices of cucumber for the wheels.
2. Cut a small piece off each slice and stand them, two either side, against the sides of the orange.

nutty soldiers

grass dragonfly

shell person

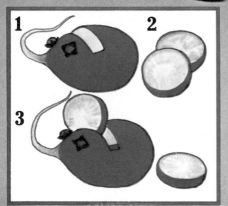

The mice

Cut the green leaves off two of
the radishes, but leave the wispy
roots. Wash and dry them.
1. Stick in cloves for the eyes.
Cut a small slot in the top of
each radish with the knife.
2. Cut slices from another
radish.
3. Stick them into the slots you
have cut to make the ears.

The cart driver

1. Cut a slice off the top and
bottom of the carrot. Stick in
cloves for eyes. Cut out a slice for
the mouth and fit in a half slice of
radish.
2. Cut a scallion into four
lengths. Make a hole either side of
the carrot with the matchstick.
3. Fit the arms, by pushing a clove
through a length into each hole.

Putting it all together

Put the mice in front of the
orange. Place two pieces of
scallion on the top of the
orange for the legs. Place the
carrot on top of them. Finally,
put the top of a radish on the
carrot, as a hat.

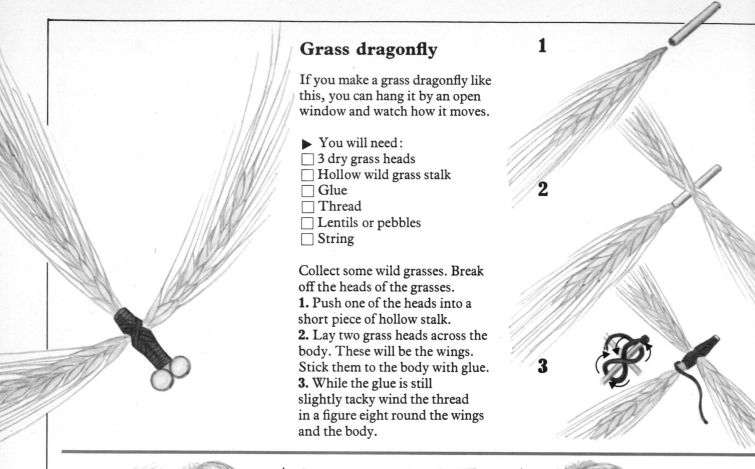

Grass dragonfly

If you make a grass dragonfly like this, you can hang it by an open window and watch how it moves.

▶ You will need:
☐ 3 dry grass heads
☐ Hollow wild grass stalk
☐ Glue
☐ Thread
☐ Lentils or pebbles
☐ String

Collect some wild grasses. Break off the heads of the grasses.
1. Push one of the heads into a short piece of hollow stalk.
2. Lay two grass heads across the body. These will be the wings. Stick them to the body with glue.
3. While the glue is still slightly tacky wind the thread in a figure eight round the wings and the body.

1

2

3

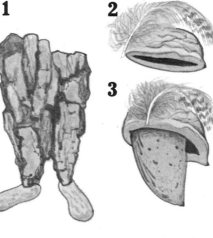

Nutty soldiers

▶ You will need:
☐ Pieces of bark
☐ Nutshells
☐ Whole nuts – almond, hazel nut
☐ Leaf or small flat shell
☐ Dried grass or feather
☐ Small twigs
☐ Glue
☐ Knife
☐ Plasticine

1

2

3

Trim the bark to make a body shape.
1. Glue the bark to the two nutshells for the feet. If it won't balance properly, stick some plasticine underneath.
2. Glue the feather or dried grass onto a half walnut shell to make the helmet plume.
3. Then glue the whole nut into this walnut helmet.

4

5

6

Now glue the head to the body.
4. On the left-hand side of the body, glue either a leaf or a shell for the shield.
5. Cut small slots at the top and bottom of a small nutshell.
6. Fit the twig for the weapon in the slots.
Glue the nutshell to the body.

4

4. Stick lentils or tiny pebbles on the top of the head for eyes. You will need to smother them with glue, so that they stick firmly. Wind one end of some string behind the wings and hang the dragonfly up by the other end.

Stone animals

You can make all sorts of strange animals simply by gluing stones of different shapes and sizes together. Collect various kinds of stones and wash them thoroughly (see page 5). Play around with them and see what animal shapes you can make.

▶ You will need:
☐ Stones of various sizes
☐ Strong glue

When you are pleased with a shape glue the parts together. First glue the head to the body. Then glue on the eyes, nose, ears and tail.

Shell person

▶ You will need:
☐ Two rounded shells for feet
☐ Large shell for body
☐ Glue
☐ Tape
☐ Plasticine
☐ Small pebbles or lentils for eyes
☐ Small shells for nose and mouth
☐ Poster paint and paintbrush

1

2

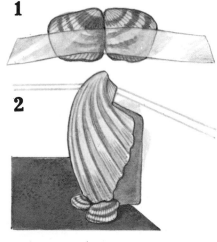

1. Place the two rounded shells side by side on your work surface and hold them in place with tape.
2. Glue the large shell onto the feet. You will probably need to stand it up against the wall with some plasticine while the glue dries.

3

4

3. Then stick on the nose and the mouth.
4. Paint the pebbles, or lentils, white, with black dots for the pupils.
Glue them in place.
(If you can't find a large shell it's worth asking at a fish store if you may have a scallop like the one in the photograph.)

Nature collage

How many creatures can you see in this picture? You can make a splendid scene with all sorts of bits and pieces picked up on a country walk—pine cones and grass for hedgehogs, cones and feathers for birds, and little pebbles with stick legs for sheep.

To make your own collage, paint in the background first. Then use strong clear glue to stick on the 'scenery'—bits of bark, moss, gravel and dried leaves. Finally, glue on your creatures.